Voice of the Cross

(A Play)

Epie Ananfah Eponsime

Miraclaire Publishing LLC
Yaounde / Kansas City (MO)

Published by

MIRACLAIRE PUBLISHING LLC

Yaounde, Cameroon
P.O. Box 8616, Yaounde 14, Centre Region, Cameroon

Kansas City, (MO) USA
8400 East 92 Terrace, Kansas City, MO 64138, USA
Website: www.miraclairebooks.com
Email: info@miraclairebooks.com

ISBN-13: 978-0615578163
ISBN-10: 0615578160

© 2011 Miraclaire Publishing
Epie Ananfah Eponsime

Dedication

To

Malike Okole Cecilia
My mother and friend

"Never forget that as creators of literary works you also have the obligation to bridge the wide gap that separates our world into two: one inhabited by a handful of excessively rich and arrogant individuals, and the other by the majority of the downtrodden, the wretched of the earth"

+Christian Cardinal Tumi
Archbishop of Douala

The true hero is the one who takes an uncompromising stand to pressure life and the integrity of men.

Professor Kashim Ibrahim Tala

CHARACTERS:

Ngome: The Rev. Pastor
Fomum: A Primary School Teacher

Papa Ewane ⎫
Ma Ewane ⎬ Ngome's Parent

Ngonde ⎫
Chucks – Berry ⎬
Baggareur ⎬ Ngome's friends
Ijengele ⎬
Ebong ⎭
Mechane: Ngome's wife
Mr. Ekema: Primary School Teacher.
X – Minister
M.P
Principal
D.M
Abunaw: Theologian
First Elder
Second Elder
Boy
Girl
Drunk
Baba: Sorcerer

CONTENTS

ACT ONE

SCENE I

Papa Ewane's residence. We find him seating in his parlour anxiously waiting for dinner.

Papa Ewane: I say-eh nya Ngom, is my supper not ready? Listen woman, my passionate patience is satiating.

Ma Ewane: I know dear, just spare me five more minutes and it shall be well. I am struggling to spice up your kwangkwalang with some obstacles.

Papa Ewane: Obstacles or no obstacles, kindly bring my soup here, nonsense. This woman doesn't know that a hungry man is an angry man and a madman if it is not controlled properly.

Ma Ewane: Please sweetie, your rib is coming oh.

Papa Ewane sings a song to distract himself.

Papa Ewane: Hmehme who will help me
Hme oh hme who will help me
Every good work has a good pay
Every bad work has a bad pay
Oh o who will help me
Hme o hme who will help me

Hot tears run down his cheeks as he nods his head several times.

Papa Ewane: Mbale, this woman will kill me. What on earth are you still doing in that kitchen.

Ma Ewane: (*placing the food on the ground*). This is your food my dear. Bon appétit.

Papa Ewane smiles and dives on the meal with a lot of zeal. The kwangkwalang contains a lot of pepper, thus causing his body to release liquid through every of his outlets. As he rounds up with the supper, Papa Ewane could not contain the heat in the house.

Papa Ewane: (*standing on his veranda*). No need to stroll. Ma Ewane has modelled my day. I see no need going to that old mokussa's place. A woman who can cook and dance makossa very well can win any man, no matter how hard he is.

Papa Ewane calls for his wife and both go to bed to conclude the supper with serious makossa.

SCENE II

A local public school. Ngome and other classmates are receiving lessons from their head teacher.

Mr. Ekema: Good morning class.

Pupil's: Good morning sir.

Mr. Ekema: I wish to teach you something new this day. It is called Career Orientation. What would you like to become in future? Kindly raise your finger for we are not in that njangi house in Yaounde where traitors defend their private interest.

Ngonde: Sir, I want to become a Treasurer. I have realized that Treasurers are very rich people.

Ngome interrupts Ngonde's explanation by standing up.

Mr. Ewane: Are you insane? Sit down you scallywag.

Ngome: I want to be a Reverend Pastor. This is because the pastoral field is highly beneficial.

Mr. Ekema: What! This child is a wizard. Regardless of your atrocities in this village, the only thing you can think of is to rob God.

Ngome: I want to become a Pastor. Pastors are never arrested for stealing or becoming rich through ill-gotten wealth.

Mr. Ekame: Let me advise you Ngome. You must change if you intend to become a Reverend Pastor. If you don't, Bakossi will forever regret giving birth to a criminal of a pastor as yourself. Diésé.

Ngome sits down and nodding his head at such embarrassment.

SCENE III

An outlet of the school compound. Ngome and other classmates are leaving the school..

Ngome: Did you hear the way Mr. Ekema cassayed my moral in class today.

Ngonde: By their fruits we shall know them. Listen friend, a gorilla and monkey may claim oneness. A monkey will always remain what it is and vice versa

Ngome: What do you mean?

Ngonde: My words are plain. When we see a cutlass, let's call it a cutlass. When we try calling it a knife, our minds will be at war.

Ngome: Spare me those archaic idioms. What is your comment about me?

Ngonde: It is obvious. You are the famous kite.

Ngome: I should have known better. So you are one of my hidden enemies? You cannot deny it.

Ngonde: If you care you can say whatever you wish to say. Let me tell you the truth, a friend who always expose your bad side to you is your best friend.

Ngome: Go away from here you traitor. Today marks the end to our friendship. I advise you to be very careful whenever you come across my territory.

Ngonde: That's alright good friend. A solution to a problem will always lie on the nature of that problem. Have a nice day. (*Moves ahead*)

Ngome: Go and sit down you hanging bat. Thank your stars that I am in a good mood, else Forchive will print bold your epitaph one of these days. Nonsense.

Exit both

SCENE IV

Papa Ewane's Residence. Papa Ewane is sitting on his veranda. Besides his leg is a four battery radio from which he is carefully listening to the five O'clock news. In the process, papa Ewane brings out his cup of wisdom and pours a good quantity in his palm which looks appetizing as he inhales it.

Papa Ewane: Wo-wo, the kangwa Mami Okafor has put in this taaku is horrible. (*hitting his forehead*) My eyes ho.

    Enter Chucks-berry

Chucks-berry: Good evening Sa Ngom

    Papa Ewane lifts up his head, inhales some good quantity of snuff.

Papa Ewane: (*in a calm voice*) ámuan, epébuammor.

Chucks-berry: Is Ngome at home.

Papa Ewane: Wusai, do you see him like someone who can be in the house at this hour of the day... Mbale that child is a failure.

Chucks-berry: Thank you papa.

Papa Ewane: Waka soffri – eh.

Chuck-berry. Yes papa

Papa Ewane: This thing that we call snuff can be dangerous. It has held me bound for thirty five years without relaxation. I am very sure of the fact that the money I have spent on snuff can build me a four rooms and a parlour. Tobacco is a very bad thing to associate with. Oh God. I pray that my progeny will not inherit this tobacco gene from me.

Enters Ngome. Ngome is singing the famous one love from Robert Nesta Marley.

Papa Ewane: Who is that madman singing into my compound as if he is void of parental training?

Ngome: It is me papa, your illustrious son.

Papa Ewane: Háa Ngome. So you are the one. This your rascalic attitude is developing to madness. Oh. Chai á sa Diob.

Ngome: Don't worry papa, your son is fine (*lifting up his two hands*).

Papa Ewane: A young man came in search of you some few minutes ago but could not lay his eyes on your doglike nature.

Ngome: Don't worry papa, I know what he is looking for. He wants kaya.

Papa Ewane: What is kaya?

Ngome: Some devotees call it gay or the golden leaf from Jah.

Papa Ewane: (*Raising up his hand*) Leave this place my friend. Nonsense.

    Exit Ngome.

Papa Ewane: What have I landed myself into? Oh God help me.

Exits.

ACT TWO

SCENE I

A path leading to Ngome's residence. Enter Ngome and Chucks-berry

Chucks- berry: High ray – Bob.

Ngome: Yeh - mbombo. How are you doing today Mr. Berry?

Chucks-berry: I have been in total starvation since morning. I have not been able to burn a single bundle of instruct.

Ngome: Where are you heading to right away?

Chucks-berry: Terre of course. I might be fortunate to meet accomplice there.

Ngome: That cannot be possible. Have you forgotten I am the only martyr who supplies chemical around this region?

Chucks-berry: Of course I know. Have you some instruct with you.

Ngome: Are you insane, do you want the police to arrest me. Just go to terre - and I will be with you in half an hour.

Chucks-berry: Are you sure?

Ngome: Fear not. Tell the others I am going to join
them within the twinkling of an eye.

Chucks- berry: Be as fast as the word else we die of
starvation.

Exit chucks- berry.

Ngome: This business is lucratively risky. Everything in
life entails a lot of risk, for without risk, no
one can boast of greatness. Money is money,
regardless of the source; I will enrich myself
to the brim.

Exit.

SCENE II

*An old abandoned stucco. Enter chucks – berry,
bagarreur and Ijengele.*

Chucks-berry: What on earth has been keeping Ngome
for so long. Are you sure Angelina is around?

Bagarreur: Who are you asking such a stupid question?
Are you not the one who gave us all the
assurance and hopes we desperately need at
this dying time.

Chucks-beery: If I be don gay, I for talk say my eyes them make mistake. I saw Ngome and he promised coming here within the twinkle of an eye.

Bagarreur: Je n'aime pas this. He should do his possible best and be here in five minutes time; else, I am on for Jahman's establishment.

Ijengele: Jahman! Does he possess quantity gay?

Bagarreur: Are you a new Rastafarian in town. Jahman has been an expert in this business ever since he was a green Lion cap. Veil him and discover that he can distinguish chemical from bahama grass with his bare hands.

Ijengele: I wash hand give Jahman.

Enter Ngome. All three stand to welcome their Lion heart.

Ngome: I am very sorry répé. You are aware of the fact that only Lion hearts can bring chemicals into Sandi Arabia.

Ijengele: Na true papi. There is nothing on earth without limitations, even capitalism.

Chucks-berry: Excellently correct Dr. Ijengele. Can you remember what Peter Lambo said in his tracks?

Ijengele: What came out of his atomic bomb?

Bagarreur: My brain is never norm when it comes to such. The Mboko-Icon, General Peter R. said *La même cause produit Le meme effet*, meaning the thing wey ido caca nayigo do caffé.

Ijengele: He also said, "no matter how long the night will be, the sun will finally rise".

Chucks-berry: That Mongolian is truly an Icon. I also heard him say *envoyé tous le monde a kondengi*

Ngome: Stop blowing Mandela's trumpet. This icon has influenced history, when are you going to do that as well. It pays to sing an infamous song to spend hellish years in Robben Island. One day, awards will visit honey like bees in the guise of human right activist.

Bagarreur: Ngome give me two mbom, soifness di come kill me.

Ngome distributes the wee to all of them. They carefully fold pencil-like bundles and smoke with a lot of ambiance. Ngome's bundle is the biggest among them.

Ijengele: (*Pretending to be fastidious*) Please Bob-Ngomi, can you lend me a single bundle of gay. *Je suis pieceless and I need for jerm for last heure*.

Ngome: No worry yourself for story with Ngombe.

Ijengele: Sorry for me Ngome, a beggar has no choice. I go manage anything wey you givam, even half mbom.

Ngome: I get na my last gay for sharp. Tie heart.

Ijengele: Na why me a no like this kaya them for one. One hundred for quartier. With just ecole-tan a kumbe and they will bring it to me well sealed. That one fit last me for two weeks. Tos me your jerm Bagarreur.

Exit all.

SCENE III

The market square. A young man is helplessly sleeping beside an Iroko tree situated at the centre of the square. His indecent act automatically draws the attention of Mr. Ekema.

Mr. Ekema: I say eh, who is this child sleeping in the open air at midi. (*Touching the sleeper*) Why are you sleeping on the road my dear? Who is your father and what is your name?

Ijengele: (*Unfolding his hidden face*) Na weti be your problem Prof. You no fit mind your own business. I beg choose me dibongo.

Chucks-berry pops in from the eastward end of the market square. Walking as if there is a heavy load on his legs, chucks inevitably captures Mr. Ekema's attention.

Mr. Ekema: (*shouting*) Chucks – berry! Why are you walking like that?

Chucks-berry: I feel as if the ground is farther than what I use to see and know. Oh! Prof, this world is truly turning around but we don't know how.

Mr. Ekema takes a bold step towards him.

Mr. Ekema: Hush! You have been in the wee estate, too bad, too too bad. I learnt garri is the cure to wee drunkenness. Let me get you some

Chucks-berry: Je veux tue, je veux tue, je veux tue. Licence et maîtrise en Droit, sans bolo, sans nuriture, ça c'est quel genre de vive. Ah, ah, vraiment je veux put an end pour cette misery.

Mr. Ekema returns carrying a bowl of soaked garri

Mr. Ekema: Here is your cooler.

Chucks-berry: God will tremendously bless you, you will live longer than Methuselah
.

Mr. Ekema: This is interesting! So you are this intelligent and extremely bilingual? I overheard you scattering French in the air like an embodiment of distinctive intelligence

Chucks-berry: Let me advise you Prof, when you find a man in a situation, be it positive or negative, be very careful to draw hasty conclusions. I distinctively grabbed a maitrise en droit at the age of twenty four, toil into various villages to see if it can be useful. Do you know what I discovered?

Mr.Ekema: Except you tell me. Maitrise – Berry.

Chucks-berry: This hand washes this hand while this hand washes this…

Mr.Ekema: Hand.

Chucks-berry: That is the thesis I came out with for the past twelve years of my research. A tycoon told me, thirty two years is the limit, yes thirty two years. With such piercing words, looking back to my perilous suffering to attain this, I definitely saw how maitrise can be useless without an opening for it to be applicable.

Ijengele: Exactly. Listen Prof, when Berry was born, it rained so heavily. When he enrolled into the primary and secondary lewa, it rained cats, dogs and pigs. When he graduated from the university, everything became operation thunder storm. Now with maitrise en droit at score 2, this boy is seeing stars. Now tell me why such a person will not have a reason to spark up a revolution in his pays. If you hear a river making noise, you must understand there are stones in it. Ijengele has made his point.

Mr. Ekema: Listen maitrise – Berry, in order to succeed in Rome, you must do what the Romans do.

Chucks-berry: And if you have not the Roman-nationality, how then can you understand, cope and enjoy the benefits of Rome such that you can conveniently do what other Romans are doing.

Mr. Ekema: Sell farms, sell plots and meet me with cash in the dungeon, and I will expose you to extra-ordinary Romans who will hand you the Roman Passport.

Chucks-berry: Listen and listen well. I am farmless and plotless, you hear me so. Had it been I never sold them to attain maitrise, maitrise would not have been stinking in my pocket at score 2.

Mr. Ekema: Please accept my condolence. Let me get you a spoon.

Berry's hands were better-off in this occasion. On the appearance of Mr, Ekema, Berry had swallowed every grain with his bare hands.

Mr. Ekema: (*In a frightful mood*) Where is the garri?

Chucks-berry: Digesting by now.

Mr. Ekema: This is dangerous. Wee is the worst thing any human being can engage himself into. Listen maitrise – Berry, be very careful, else you destroy your lungs or become mad someday as a result of wee.

Chucks-berry: I am very sorry prof. Frustration carried me on its vulture wings and landed me into the waiting hands of Ngome, who introduced me to wee smoking. (*Coughs for a while and stops*) Oh Ngome! Oh frustration! I regret the day you introduced me to wee, (*crying aloud*) who is going to help me eh! I am dying of tuberculosis as a result of wee. Chai frustration! Frustration! Frustration! You can cause one to link to misery and destroy the bright future God graciously gave him. Very soon, the law of Kamer will drop on Louise number sixteen, the architect of my frustration. Listen prof, if you want to know the situation and the solution to my country, go and study the French Revolution of 1789.

Mr. Ekema: Exactly.

Ijengele: Confirm.

Exit all.

SCENE IV

Papa Ewane's residence. Papa Ewane is complaining bitterly about Ngome's rascalic behaviours. His wife struggles to calm him by picking invisible dirt from his head, chin and his shirt.

Papa Ewane: Nya-ngome, this your son is going to seize oxygen from me. I am suspecting that blood because my family has never given birth to such a zombie.

Mr Ewane: Please sweety (*picks an invisible dirt from his chin*) stop being pessimistic and judging from a wrong direction.

Papa Ewane: Why shouldn't I, tell me the truth, did you….

Mr Ewane: (*stands up*) What do you mean? You took me from my father as a virgin and you know it. No one is in keeping of any spare key to my paradise except you. God!

Papa Ewane: Na talk that.

Ma Ewane: Is that all you can say.

Papa Ewane: Yes. My blood is not in that iguana.

Ma Ewane: Listen dear, he is suffering from adolescence

Papa Ewane: Adolescence my bald head! Adolescence my hunch-back! I have done virtuously everything I needed to do. Listen, that boy will never change.

Ma Ewane: Are you cursing your son.

Papa Ewane: Far be it from me. Listen, no matter how loud a crocodile struggles to shout, it will never swallow the hippopotamus. Any amount of rain fall will always remain meaningless to the frightful spots of a Leopard.

Ma Ewane: (*Sitting*) Listen dear, adolescence stage is a time every parent should control their children with a lot of technicality. If they don't, such children will end up as he-goats and heat-wild horses. I strongly believe that with time he will definitely change.

Papa Ewane: Ngome is really a disgrace to my family. (*Crying*) What am I going to do? Oh! A sa Diob. Truly a thief is never as ashamed as the father-and other family members and friends related to the thief.

Ma Ewane: (*Scolding him*) stop crying my dear, such attitudes are normal with children of such age group.

A knock at the dear. Enter Mr.Ekema.

Mr. Ekema: Good evening Sango – Ewane.

Papa Ewane remain silent.

Ma Ewane: Good evening Milied.

Mr. Ekema: Are you aware of the fact that Ngome now trades on wee? Ijengle and Chucks-berry are helplessly lying in the hospital as a result of this infamous trade.

Papa Ewane: (*claps his hands*). These boys are about twice the age of Ngome. How can Ngome influence an intellectual such as Chucks-berry who is far older than Ngome. Is it because of his height?

Mr Ekema: I am also surprised at what my eyes and ears have seen and heard this day.

Papa Ewane: (*shouting*) Ngome, Ngome.

Ngome: Papa

Papa Ewane: So you now trade on wee? Answer me you scallywag. (*Grabs him by the neck*). I assure you, if you do not change, your name will be a taboo in this Bakossi land.

Ngome: Stop embarrassing me papa. I don't understand what you guys are talking about.

Papa Ewane: Haa! So you still have the impetus to talk, you have the guts to justi...

(*chokes*).

Ma Ewane: Please for water.
Papa Ewane falls on the floor, holds his neck and chest as he coughs continuously. Struggling to raise him
Please hurry, hurry with that water.

Papa Ewane stretches himself in the hands of ma Ewane, groans and ends it all. We hear a serious wailing from Ma Ewane and Mr. Ekema while Ngome stands at akimbo as if he is in a dream world.

Exit all.

ACT THREE

SCENE I

At the Funeral. There is an outstanding crowd in Papa Ewane's residence. At the centre of the compound is a canopy with the inscription "Sumediang". Papa Ewane's remains are placed on a table in front of sumediang. The whole compound is saturated with people tying folded loin cloths round their waist.

Enter Pastor Ediage.

Pastor: Peace be with you all.

Mourners: And also with you.

Pastor Ediage: My dear people of God, we are gathering here today for a single reason. Mr. Ewane is to be sent off today to a land nobody knows, except God. We are all aware of Mr. Ewane who extremely committed himself to pay all his church contributions as Galatians 6:6 says. Before we proceed, I will like us to sing song number 10 in the funeral program.

Mourners open their funeral programs and jointly sing.

> I see before me just two wills
> The will of God and the enemy's

No other will besides this two;
I'll do your will.

I will not bring in my own will
For my will would be the enemy's
I take your will my Lord for mine,
I'll do your will.

I give myself to seek your will.
In all I think and say and do,
And when it's found my choice is made,
I'll do your will.

Z.T.F

Pastor Ediage: Had it been it was left to our own wills, Mr. Ewane would have been alive till date. Unfortunately for us, the will of God is the best. Offertory, offertory, offertory.

A communicant comes forward with a huge basket and flashes it to every mourner such that they can be opportuned to support the work of God. As the basket goes round, the amount of money seem insignificant to the Pastor whose smiling face falls with a single gaze at the basket.

Pastor Ediage: Please some able youths should help us carry the remains to the grave.

Six youths comes up, carry the coffin and lower it in Papa Ewane's new house.

Pastor Ediage: This is the final destination for every carnal thing that embodies our beloved brother, father, husband and friend. Death has no respect for mortals. (*Carries a handful of dust and dumps it in the grave*). From dust man was made and unto dust man must return.

There is a serious weeping from mourners.

Pastor Ediage: (*prays*) Oh Lord we thank you for willingly taking our brother away from our midst. We thank you for his endless efforts to see your work succeed. We beg you to receive his spirit, and may his soul rest in perfect peace. Amen.

Mourners: Amen.

Pastor Ediage: In the name of the father, and of the son and of the Holy Spirit. Amen

Mourners: Amen.

Pastor Ediage: Is there any announcement.

Enter Pa Ejedepang Ngalame.

Ejedepang Ngalame: Yes Pastor. We di beg say make no man no go. We get plenti chop and mimbo for all man for here. If you no flop, ask for more chop. People wey them dig grave, wuna go chop for kona grave while the rest them go chop for round table.

Pastor Ediage: Please we need a word of condolence from Papa Ewane's intimate friend.

Enter Pa Ekema Coco

Pa Ekema Coco: Mr. Ewane was a very good and humble man, always smiling whenever he comes across friends and enemies too. Mr. Ewane was a Pelican who could climb on an ant and it will not die. This road is for everybody. Today is Ewane's day, tomorrow might be the wife; in fact she is not even well.

Mourners: Bitter truths….very bitter truths in life.

Pastor Ediage: While the grave diggers cover the grave, join me in signing song number 1of the program as we look forward to item eleven and jecking-neck.

Mourners: Very important….very essential

Mourners join him to sing the song.

> Mon Dieu, plus prés de toi,
> Plus prés de toi
> C'est le mot de ma foi
> Plus pres detoi
> Dans le jour oul'épreuve

Déborde comme un fleuve
Garde – moi prés de toi,
Plus prés de toi

Plus prés de toi toujours
Plus prés de toi
Donne moi ton secours
Soutiens ma foi
Que satané se dechaine,
Ton amour me ramène
Toujours plus prés de toi
Plusprés de toi

Mon Dieu plus prés de toi
Dans le désert
J'ai vu plus prés de toi
Ton cielouvert.
Pèlerin, bon courage !
Ton chant brave l'orage….
Mon Dieu plus prés de toi.
Plus prés de toi.

CHATELANAT.

SCENE II

At about half past five, a group of people on their way out of Papa Ewane's compound.

X-Minister: I never expected Mr. Ewane of all people to die so suddenly. Truly, life is shorter than our very imagination about it – dwarfism. Many people are saying that alum and atog are responsible for his death. Oh God, change our ébúmé and deliver us from this great ebébtéd.

M.P.: What do you expect? In this life, you must belong in order to safeguard your existence. I am a devotee of ahon and I strongly believe no one born of a woman can kill me before my time. Haven't you heard people call me the Orange-root? This is me nhon Ebang (beating his chest) the Orange-root himself.

X-Minister: I don't love such groups. I learned they operate in the metaphysical realm with ease. No one can belong to such groups without knowledge of witchcraft. I will never shelter from rain where I clearly know I will not be able to sleep, even though people say 'a beggar has no choice'

M.P: Well, that's your own point of view. Now I understand your sudden epileptic mood resulting from Mr. Ewane's untimely death. Can you remember what I told you in Ngola?

X-Minister: You told me many things while in Ngola. Can you please remind me of what you intend to remind me of?

M.P: Why not. If not of our presence, Elong would have been disgraced in Abakwa. When that atmosphere was handed to him as controleur, we extra-ordinarily displayed our powers, commanding the rain to obey us and it did. Listen man, it is all your benefit to join the winning team and free yourselves from fear. You are an X-Minister and we do not know you because you are titleless as far as our clan is concerned. How gracious it is when you are recognized as an elite and a nhon in our clan.

On Hearing this, the X – Minister unintentionally knocks his leg on a stone.

X-Minister: I don't know when roads will ever be glassy in this Tombel town. Everywhere stones, everywhere stones.

M.P: You had the opportunity to cause these stones to disappear once and for all and you jeopardized it with, who knows. How I wish I were in your shoes then.

X-Minister: what have you done in your present shoe. This is a third time you are wearing the same shoe which is not truly yours but the people, very contrary to chef de block.

M.P: This shoe is mine even if I wear it a tenth time. It is as a result of my capability to manage this shoe, reasons why the people have surrendered the shoe to me as mudgageur numéro un.

X-Minister: Are you sure of what you are saying.

M.P: Perfectly sure. Don't mind what bias sorcerers say about my wearing of this shoe. They claim it is the L'oustien chap who pacified my journey to the land of collaboration and distinctive submission. Man, I advise you to play the patient dog, for you might be fortunate to eat the fattest bone after the fastest dogs must have munched the juicy but rotten flesh.

X-Minister: Wearing this sans confiance, I am praying so day and night. Do you think I am a fool to remain in Ngola? I definitely know what I am doing. There is a saying that "if you see a man walking, he definitely knows where he is heading to except he is a madman". The Moungorian democrat embraced the cold in Sabaria, preferable to the guillotine and finally found favour as chief sparrow hawk at the age of 70 something. Retirement is powerless over that kudos chaser.

Their discussion is interrupted by a drunk from the funeral as well.

Enter drunk.

Drunk: Wow! Vois L'ancien Ministre, oui, l'ancien ministre, sans gardien. A vos orders monsieur le ministre.

X-Minister: Who are you referring such insults to?

Drunk: We are just from Mr. Ewane's funeral and you saw him discern into the world unknown with all his titles. Man-made titles are as worthless as the word. Yesterday, you were with a convoy demanding applauses from the downtrodden. The reverse is manifesting itself today, no doubt we have no option but to call you L'ancien minister after the news at five has been broadcast nationwide.

X-Minister: (*Rising up his right hand*). Be careful, else I am going to deal with you, regardless of your state of drunkenness. Nyamkusu.

Drunk: What! Deal with me! (*Sighs*) Look at this victim of appellé á d'autre function.

X-Minister: Shut up! Shut up! Shut up!

Drunk: I won't. I believe it is high time you understand that all human beings are equal before God. You will be as helpless as the word on the judgment seat of Christ, reasons being your negligence in associating with the born again way of life in Christ Jesus. I am struggling to become one; else drunkenness takes me to the waiting hands of hell.

M.P: I perceive some sense in what this drunk is saying. I am very grateful of the fact that "appéllé á d'autre function" is powerless over me. I am not scared of the national broadcast at 5p.m, very dangerous and shocking to its victims. Five years is my challenge and I must plan my life before it cease to exist. A goat will always eat where it is tied. As for becoming a born again, I am already one in our church, even though people criticize my loyalty to ahon society and at the same time an excellent devotee to the church. Anyway, a broken glass must have shades of various shapes and sizes.

Drunk: I assure you Mr. Ahon member, if you do not forsake that fetish secret society and surrender your totality to Christ wholeheartedly, you will definitely go to hell. There are many of your kind who are devotees to deferent secret satanic societies, yet identify themselves with the church by contributing huge sums to distract them from your satanic nature. Listen, your money and your contributions cannot and will never save you. Unless you repent of all your sins of stealing, killing, lies telling, greed, occultism, sexual immorality and envy, you will never enter heaven when you die.

X-Minister: Are you talking to us like that.

Drunk: The truth is very venomous to a guilty and an unrepentant person. Change and save your souls from going to hell.

X-Minister: Yes (*stares around*) yes, the wrong place.

M.P: If you do not leave this place now, I will make a phone call and you will forever blame yourself for saying the wrong thing at the wrong time and in the wrong place.

X-Minister: Yes (*stares around*) yes, the wrong place.

Drunk: I will. Consider what I have said, else your egg falls to the ground and becomes shades of coxcombs, with ants and flies making mockery of soiled yoke particles.

X-Minster: Go away with your stinking mouth.

M.P: Nyam.ngu.

Exit all.

SCENE III

Seven scores at hand. Ngome is now a holder of the teachers grade two certificate. Enter Ngome.

Ngome: I have served as a teacher for the past five years, yet my life seems rolling anticlockwise. Teaching is really a miserable job to dark colours. Wages and credits should be universal according to categories and not cock crowing sectors.

    Enter Fomum

Fomum: I over-heard you speaking to yourself. I hope all is well

Ngome: How can all be well when my eyes have seen my ears? We are those who train future academics of this African in miniature, putting in our all as midwives to deliver citizens from ignorantio. Truly, this contemporary society forgets to understand that grass always germinates with the first rain.

Fomum: Why are you being pessimistic about such a noble profession? As mortals, we must be contented with whatever God gives us. Do you think our employer is that wicked to give us incomes which won't suit our standards and meet all our needs?

Ngome: I am sure you are in a dream world. Listen prof, I am an only child in my family, the only working class and caretaker of the same family. All the eyes of my family members are fixed towards my meaningless income. This income is void of out station and in station credits and allowances. Is it possible for one to cope in such a situation if not of overdraft and loan?

Fomum: Don't worry.

Ngome: Those words exiled the Germans to millions of miles away from Kamerun.

Fomum: Please manage what you have, and God will bless the fruits of your labour.

Ngome: In my grave.

Fomum: While breathing Oxygen.

Ngome: (*smiles*) how many children have you?

Fomum: None.

Ngome: None.

Fomum: Yes none.

Ngome: And your brothers, they are serious directors in outstanding offices due to Munafoncha and Achidifru pipelines. These pipelines remind me of grievous 61, abominable 72, disastrous 82 and horrific 96. Listen man, have you a mastery of Judas Iscariot's experience? He hanged himself because he was neither a bird nor an animal. Beware brotherman for Judas never lived to enjoy those thirty pieces of silver.

Fomum: Why are you so coded in your speeches?

Ngome: Because I understand why you confidentially blow words with such temerity. Listen man, it is only he who wears the shoe, knows where it pinches. I am going to quit teaching immediately I discover a lucrative job from any N.G.O. As for my two kids, I prefer their engagement into two white V's beneath blue cap than being a teacher for seventy years.

Fomum: Are you serious about what you are saying?

Ngome: Of course I am. Can you imagine Major Owona Yokono, an F.S.L.C holder, owning a Mercedes-Benz?

There is a knock at the door. Enter Ebong with a letter in his hands.

Ebong: Ngome good news, good news Ngome, good good news.

Ngome: Good news! I can't wait to hear it.

Ebong: The church needs people to train as pastors. I am very willing to write the competitive entrance examination. What of you, are you interested as well?

Ngome: You need not ask. My opinion is plain. I am going to write that exam with all my soul.

Fomum: (*embarrassed*) Are you going to abandon teaching?

Ngome: Without an iota of regrets, I will. I wish you the best in that your job massi. What is the essence of working without a substantial wage to solve all your problems? I am gone for pastoral business.

Fomum: You should be careful not to join this core in order to maximize profit. If your intention of joining the pastoral core is to make money, I assure you your end might be disastrous.

Ngome: Haa! A wasp is truly different from a yellow jacket. North westerners are very sensitive when money matters are concerned. I think your mother should be investigated concerning your true father.

Fomum: Be careful-oh! Ngome else you destroy your destiny. Don't follow the ways of those who are experts in distorting the beautiful reflection on a mirror.

Ngome: Come out plain my friend.

Fomum: If you know you have been called to become a pastor, do that without reservation. If the reverse is true, I plead with you not to dare God's patience. If you are reasonable enough, you will realize that it is more philosophical to build than to destroy.

Ngome: Stop weeping more than the bereaved. Let's allow this topic to the ticking of the clock. Sooner than later you will testify of my reverendship.

Fomum: I wish you the best.

Ngome: May your elbow graciously grease continuously, you are indeed a moralist but remember, morality can't afford anything from the market. We badly need money to survive.

Exit Fomum.

Ebong: Don't mind that Fomum, he claims to be too religious as if his father was a reverend pope.

Ngome: Point of correction. We call the pope His holiness and not reverend. You have changed my mood this day. May God continue to bless these feet of yours which always come along with good news.

Ebong: Merci.

Ngome: I am already feeling the pastoral spirit in my bones. Thank you once more for giving me a boat.

Exit all

SCENE IV

Fomum's Residence. A beautiful compound surrounded with flowers and fruits. At the eastward end of the compound is an apple tree with extremely ripe fruits. Fomum is sitting under the apple tree, glancing through the Holy Bible with a lot of smiles. At the entrance to his compound, we find a boy and a girl walking majestically into his compound with treasure bags.

Boy: Good evening Sir.

Fomum: Thank you my dear. Can I be of help to you?

Boy: Sir, I plead to share the gospel with you. Will you mind sparing us five to ten minutes of your precious time?

Fomum: Why not (*points at a bench beside him*) make yourselves comfortable.

Boy: Please let's pray.

    Girl leads the prayer till the end and all shout Amen.

Boy: I will like us to look at the gospel according to Saint John. Let's reads from John chapter 3:16. It reads "For God so loved the world that He gave His only begotten son, such that whosoever believeth in Him, will not perish but have eternal life".

Fomum: I am aware of that. I was born a Christian till this moment. When you came in, didn't you find me reading the Holy Scriptures.

Boy: Yes we did.

Fomum: So, if I say I am a Christian then I must be telling the gospel truth.

Girl: I wish to ask you a question sir.

Fomum: Go ahead my dear.

Girls: Have you truly repented of all your sins and forsaken them.

Fomum: What do you mean? God's grace is sufficient for us. There is no one who can be sin free. When we sin, we beg God for forgiveness and he will always do so because He is a compassionate God.

Girl: I will like us to read from the book of Romans chapter 6: 1 – 2. It reads "well then, should we continue sinning such that God can show us more and more grace? Of course not! Since we have died to sin, how can we continue to live in it". The Bible also says in the book of revelation that "nothing impure shall ever enter the kingdom of God. Rev.21:8. The truth is a man is qualified for the hottest part in hell with just a single sin in his life. Sin destroys and draws mortals closer to sickness and to the grave. If you are actively living in any sin, be sure of going to hell when you die".

Fomum: Are you serious.

Girl: Yes I am. You can best find this in the book of Galatians chapter 5:19 – 21 which spells out sins such as adultery, fornication, sorcery, adulatory, drunkenness, envy, anger and more others.

Fomum: What must I do to be saved, what must I do to be free from the power of sin and a sinful lifestyle.

Girl: You must humbly confess your sins to God, repent of them, forsake them with all your heart and follow Jesus at all cost.

Fomum: I want to give my life to Christ and be free from the bondage of sin. I am an adulterer, a liar and a drunk. I don't want to cheat on my wife any longer. I don't want to go to hell when I die.

Fomum kneels in front of them, repenting and regretting his past life. We find tears rolling down his checks as he prays, committing himself to abandon all his past sins and follow righteousness at all cost.

Exit all.

SCENE V

Ngome's Residence. Ngome is attentively reading a newspaper entitled "Cameroon Tribune". Of a sudden, Ebong runs into Ngome's house as if thieves were after him. Ngome immediately jump from his seat and runs in fright.

Ebong: Stop

Ngome takes a halt and turn.

Ngome: Why did you pop into my house like that?

Ebong: You have passed the competitive entrance examination into the school of Theology.

Ngome: (*crying aloud*) What! Are you serious, oh! My perilous days have come to an end.

Enter Ma Ewane.

Ma Ewane: Why are you shouting and crying.

Ngome: I have passed the entrance into the pastoral college....

Ma Ewane: No, I strongly disagree with this idea. You are already a civil servant and can't afford to abandon the civil service for an N.G.O. Are you insane?

Ngome: I am alright mama. I have decided to quit the civil service. Can you imagine that for the past five years I have been with them, my profit have been two heavy hernia operations of which I am still owing the Doctor Bate.

Ma Ewane: Listen my dear son, I am really scared of this your new decision. I am on my knees (kneels) don't run into pastoral service like that.

Ngome: (*raising her*) Trust me mama. If I can pass the examination, what then can serve as an obstacle to my new job.

Ma Ewane: I am swimming in a terrible omen. Permit my advice to penetrate your wax-like ears. It is better and most preferable to feed on poverty in a guiltless conscience. Change your opinion, persevere as a teacher and one day you will be blessed by those who have benefited from your academic store house.

Ngome: Don't worry mama. I know where I am heading to. There are many roads to Yaounde; what is important is the means to get there.

Ma Ewane: Take an old woman's advice and spare yourself from a dangerous predicament.

Ngome: Take a son's ambition and pray that he succeeds for the benefit of the whole family.

Exit Ma Ewane.

Ebong: It seems your mum is up for much quantity of sand in your garri.

Ngome: Don't you trust me? I am a hard nut to crack even though my mother claims to crack any nut. This is my God sent opportunity, and I am sure I am up to the task. God permitted me to pass this examination because he knew I am able to the task. (*Turns towards Ebong*) Have you some instruct with you.

Ebong: Of course. You are aware of the fact that I can't go along without instruct in my pocket.

Ngome: Which stuff have you, is it Bob Jahman.

Ebong: Not at all. I bought this stuff from Mr Ebonji Yesterday. He is a new Rastafarian in Ebonji who is an expert in drying instruct. He is the best Kaya seller around that region.

Enter Mechane.

Mechane: Darling, what is instruct?

Ngome: Shut up and go to the room. How dare you open your month to speak while men are discussing paramount issues?

Mechane: I am sorry dear

Ngome: You better be. (*To Ebong*) look at a woman I bought with my money. On the day of my traditional wedding, her parents thought they have seen their own biafra, and brought out women of various shapes and sizes with covered faces in order to enable me discover my wife. I gave much money and they said it wasn't enough. I added and added until I took her away like a fowl. Her family dealt with a miserable teacher as myself because I was desperately in love with their daughter. Listen Ebong, there are certain tribes in Cameroon who sell their daughters and not give them out for marriage. Please watch - out.

Exit all.

ACT FOUR

SCENE I

The Sosonya school of Theology. Ngome is standing by the window of his dormitory with his eyes fixed on the beautiful plains of the Kupe Mountain. In his hands, we find a book titled "Patience the key to a trustworthy lifestyle". He opens and closes it several times without bothering to read a page of it. Doing this, Ngome nods his head several times as if the whole world is on his head.

Ngome: This people said the pastoral program is going to last for twenty four month. I have already spent ten difficult months in this place. Oh God, how I wish these 24 months come and go within the twinkle of an eye. Oh God help me. My Patience is almost at the elastic limit.
(Removes a stick of L & B from his pocket and kisses its tip with flame).
Every day corn chaff, every day corn chaff. I am tired of eating one and the same meal every morning afternoon, evening. Last week, they willingly asked us to stave and they in turn eat from their houses and say we are going through spiritual training.
(Puffs a good quantity of smoke in the air as his head rises and falls. In the process, he noticed one of the instructors eating in front of his house).

Look at that bald head of a pastor. He cannot do without food, no doubt his stomach keeps bunging. Heavy feeder. I wonder if this bald head of a pastor ever fasted during his pastoral training. When they asked us to starve the other day, he is the one who came at the fore front and spoke eloquently with his inquisitive stomach, saying "yes you must fast in order to become very spiritual". Look at you, chewing as if you have become a pig.

There is a knock at the door. Ngome hastily drops the cigarette and crushes it with his leg.

Enter D.M.

D.M.: What are you doing here while your friends are busily praying in the Chapel? This is degrading to your career and you know it.

Ngome: I am not feeling too well. Can you please grant me two days permission? I wish to go home and treat myself with some fever grass and Ndume-worm melesin.

D.M.: No. I cannot. That's impossible. Have you forgotten that we have a big hospital in this village?

Ngome: Of course I know. But...

D.M: But what! Go and see the doctor and stop bandying words with me.

Ngome: But.

D.M: But what. Don't you realize your birth right has been sold to the church? It became ours the very day you swore loyalty to the church. You are now a slave to the church and God, the owner of the church.

Ngome: Slave.

D.M: Yes slave. Listen, you now belong to the church and you are the church's property. Do you understand?

Ngome: Who are you shouting at, are you senseless to realize that I am a grown up, a married man with children.

D.M: Who cares? The sooner you realize you are the church's property, the better for you. (*Shout*) Leave this room and join your friends in the chapel.

Ngome: Why

D.M: I want to bar the door. (*Pushing Ngome*) Please hurry, hurry and stop wasting God's time.
Ngome leaves the window and moves out
Exit all.

SCENE II

A path leading to the chapel. Ngome is strolling majestically on the story path whose side are decorated with beautiful hedges.

Ngome: This so called D.M is truly fearless. How dare him, who is he, who gave him the impetus, the guts and the temerities to shout at a onetime teacher of a public school.
(*Laughs and clap his hands*).
Life is as unpredictable as a woman. Life is truly full of surprises. Chai. The worst of it is that he is lame. He should thank his stars that I am in good mood today else I must have taught him a lesson of his life and quite this uncomfortable arena. Try that your nonsense with me next time, and I will intentionally cut off your two hands and chop off this other leg that is remaining. And you will be like an envelope, legless.

An uproar of jubilation from the chapel. Ngome runs into the chapel.

Ngome: (*to a Theologian*) what is happening here?

Theologian: Where have you been?

Ngome: That is not the answer to my question. I don't know why most of you Africans love answering questions by asking more questions.

Theologian: Alright sir, the principal is just from informing us that the big man has decided to butcher our program.

Ngome: Are you serious?

Theologian: Of course I am. As from this badge hence forth, the program will be twelve month.

Ngome: (*shouting*) Twelve months! God is not sleeping on my part. Oh Lord thank you for shortening the program that has tortured me for years to end in total penury. (*Turns to the Theologian*) hey man, what is your name.

Theologian: Abunaw Enow-eta Tabi. Tanyi

Ngome: Are you a Nigerian.

Theologian: No, I am from Bisong-Abangin Manyu division.

Ngome: That's interesting. O o oh, I was told one can use three days from Kumba to that your place during the rainy season. Where do you intend to rule after graduation?

Theologian: I am called to serve and not to rule. Any person who rules is a tyrant. All leaders are called to be servant and not rulers.

Ngome: Aright, where will you like to serve as pastor.

Theologian: Anywhere the Lord sends me. Be it a town or village and not the size of the congregation.

Ngome: Village! Definitely not. I wish to be posted to Tombel Town.

Theologian: That's very interesting. Please let's concentrate.

Ngome: concentrate.

Theologian: I need not to be disturbed any longer.

> *Enter D.M.*
> *He quietly walks towards the principal and hands him a paper.*

D.M.: Sir, so treat it with urgency.

Principal: Thanks. I am going to run my eyes through it when I get home.

D.M.: That's ok by me sir.

Ngome: What has this crawler given to the principal? Let it not be that he is trying to put stones in my garri. If he does, I will sting his life with my venom. Nonsense.

Principal: Rise up a a all of y you and le le let us pray to end this wo, wonderful session. All rise on both legs as he prays.

Exit all.

SCENE III

The Principal's Residence. The Principal is sitting on one of the three cane chairs in his parlour. In his hands, we find an envelope which looks somehow suspicious with regard to his gaze towards it.

Principal: (*Opens the letter and read*)

The D.M;
Sosonya   School   of
Theology.

Sir, with maximum respect, I humbly dish out my greetings. I wish to inform you of the rate of indiscipline in this school of God. Our young shepherds are practicing sacrilegious activities in this godly arena without a blink of fear. Sir, something should be done to save our ecclesiastic circle from future anarchy and chaos.

Thanks

Mr. Thomas Kaka Mulema.

The principal nods his head and folds the letter.

Principal: O oh God help me. What will people s s say, that I I I I tri trained arm robbers instead of good shepherds. How can I free myself from these foxes? Oh God help me.

There is a knock at the door.

Principal: God scratches matches. Who are y y you.

Enter Ngome.

Principal: What is it?

Ngome: No cause for alarm. I am here to greet you sirs, good morning.

Principal: Enhen.

Ngome: I brought you some fruits (*sends forward a black nylon paper*). Galatians 6:6 is something not to joke with in this training of ours. God will always love a cheerful giver.

Principal: (*puts on a smiling face*) thank you. You are truly a sower. I promise you, you will reap a hundred fofofofol fold.

Ngome: Thank you sir.

Principal: You are the most sensitive in a handful of your kind in this school. God Bless y you.

Ngome: Merci.

Principal: I see in you one of those who will make us proud out there in the field.

Ngome: Cock sure – sir.

Principal: Kindly do your best to defend the stamina of this ideal school of theology.

Ngome: I may.

Principal: Before your arrival, I I I have been running my eyes over a seismic letter fr fro from the D.M. From now hence forth, w w we are going to dismiss every undisciplined fellow. Do you und und under understand.

Ngome: Yes Sa'a.

Principal: Dismiss, thanks for the fruits.

Ngome: You are welcome.

Exit both.

SCENE IV

The Church Hall. Ngome is standing on the pulpit, dressed in an elegant gown. There is mighty cross on each side of his gown. Ngome's face appears more mature with a huge moustache gazing with fright.

Ngome: Five years were here and gone with my recorded services to this congregation. God is unique in his dealings, no doubt, God passionately sent me to feed his sheep in Tombel Town. Kindly join me in singing song number ten of the song book.

Congregation sings:

> Take my life and let it be
> Consecrated Lord to Thee.
> Take my moments and my days.
> Let them flow in ceaseless praise.

Ngome: This is exactly what we must do as Christians. My dear brothers and sisters of God, your life, your money, your ékokè, your nyákè and your cocoyam must be offered to God as sacrifices. I assure you, your reward is great in Heaven. Offertory. No brown coin should dare enter the offering basket.

> *Two elders step forward in red robes. Each of them stands at the extreme of the two rows, directing Christians on how to orderly go to the*

offering basket. This exercise is done perfectly to the end.

Ngome: Second round.

The elders move from bench to bench, commanding Christians with their action to run towards the money basket. This exercise is done in such a way that every Christian must be seen and those without second round will easily suffer the shock and disgrace. Painful second round come to an end.

Ngome: Third round. Please come and give cheerfully to God and to this work. God loves a cheerful giver and will greatly reward all those who give cheerfully.

A handful of well-dressed ladies and gentlemen joyfully stroll to the money-box and gives kumbaly.

Exit all.

SCENE V

The Pastor's Office. Two elders are busy counting cash

1st Elder: This harvest today is God sent.

2nd Elder: What do you mean?

1st Elder: Can't you read the signs in the air, much much money to circulate in a triangular form.

2nd Elder: How much came into your basket.

1st Elder: Long awaited 90,000frs.

2nd Elder: My basket produced 82,011frs. Many people were on your side, reasons why you defeated me at the counting point.

1st Elder: Yea. You are noted for corruption, stealing and even embezzlement. I wonder why you even had some people to give you an opportunity to realize figures due to your notoriety.

2nd Elder: Your mouth is quinine like.

1st Elder: Of course, only the truth, sincerity, consciousness and altruism can set a man free from future guilt and regret.

2nd Elder: can we play our famous game

1st Elder: Of course. Listen my dear, you can be a breather of good scent but metamorphosis over night to become a breather of massacre – nyoslikescent. I am going to slash 30,000frs form my basket. What about you.

1st Elder: 30,000frs is going to amend my perilous situation. Do you know how I struggled to be position here?, I fought so hard, gave the pastor everything I possess in order to secure this lucrative position. Did you travel through the same route as myself.

2nd Elder: Why not. You speak as if you are a novice in this game. This crook you call Pastor Ngome Paulus has taken total possession of my husband's bearded meat.

1st Elder: Eeh! So he now feeds on your husband's bearded treasure.

2nd Elder: That's a bite of his venomous deeds. Please, kindly keep this a secret. (*turn round*). He killed my husband and indirectly seized my two kids to stabilize his sexual gratification.

1st Elder: It must remain a secret. I for one am not different from you. He mans me as well and has been feeding on my husband's ruin vault. Listen, my slippery path is worn-out because of his rendezvous I reluctantly attended yesterday night.

2nd Elder: What should we do to him? Sleeping with two co-workers is offensive to womanhood. Let's eliminate him it is often said "when you have a bad leader kill him".

1st Elder: what! Are you from Babanki. It is a serious offense to kill a leader, not to mention a man of God. God who made him our shepherd will take him away at his appointed time.

2nd Elder: Please, let's hide this money as quick as possible.

Two elders collect 30,000frs each and hide in their pants.

1st Elder: Besides, for the past five years, no project, development and spiritual transformation have been realized in this church. Oh! Pastor Abel, only God alone will avenge what this descendant of Cain did to you.

There is a knock at the door. Enter Ngome.

Ngome: Oh! My sweet and dear sisters of God. How did you enjoy the service?

Elders: Wonderful and helpful is its name.

Ngome: And the offering.

1st Elder: Here it is. We consciously counted the cash and realized the sum of 11,2011frs.

Ngome: Hey don't tell me that, I hate that figure. If you rogues think you are crooks, I am going to prove to you that I am the architect of them all. My eyes were very watchful when every single C.F.A. was poured into those baskets. I devotedly counted all ten and five thousands francs note. I am not in the mood to listen to your mimbo house story. Promotion is meant for those who collaborate with me and not those who oppose me or try playing monkey tricks to betray the genuine confidence I vested upon them.

2nd Elder: Don't you trust us, Sango.

Ngome: A fool drowning in his folly will eat the delicious meal of his wife after a quarrelling session, fighting session or spotting her in an adulterous act. (*shouting*) Tell me the truth else I render you lifeless. Nonsense.

1st Elder: Stop threatening us.

Ngome: What! If you dare me one more time, I will put down this pastoral garment and prove to you that I am a chameleon.

2nd Elder: You are already one .and cannot threaten us with these scanty words of yours. You have been sleeping with us and here you are, pretending as if the genes of a fox are not running through your veins.

Ngome: That's enough woman. Have you forgotten I am your pastor?

1st Elder: Pastor indeed. Listen Mr. Pastor, a true pastor doesn't commit Adultery, stealing, killing, sorcery occultism and envy. You are an embezzler in the church and need to be exiled before destroying this rich, fertile, peaceful and productive church at the advantage of your fastidious and egocentric nature.

Before these last words could drop from her lips, Ngome brings the mouth to absolute order. Ngome's action causes 2nd Elder's attempt to escape.

Ngome: Stop there, you adulterous fellow. It is a taboo for a woman to bear the dual identity of a thief and an adulterer at the same time. (*Raising up his right hand*). Where is my money?

2nd Elder: Sang Sang Sango I I will talk.

Ngome: Speak out else I seize oxygen from you, you rebel. Nyam-nguu.

2nd Elder: We stole 30,000frs each and hid it in our pants. I, I mean my flower showed up five minutes ago and lava is seriously flowing on the money.

Ngome: Abomination! This is sacrilegious. How dare you take Holy money and keep in your abominable triangles. I am not going to touch that defiled cash. (*Turns towards 1st Elder*). Are you on that your thing as well.

No response. Her hands are still on her face.

Ngome: I am going to dismiss you all. (*Pointing at the door*) Get out of my office and never return, else you embrace your water-loo. Bloody thieves and adulterers.

Exit Elders.

Ngome: The unquenchable thirst for money is a global desire. I must meet my objectives at all cost, no matter the means. When you live in an atmosphere where survival depends on choko, collaboration, submission and identity, one is placed under no option but do what the Romans are doing in order to survive the harsh winter in Rome. A man can be as decent as decency but finally becomes an icon of indecency in an environment where all is forced to breathe the $Co2$ of indecency in order to survive. With just five years of service, I now own two large farms, buses and a very huge house. Isn't this better than teaching? If the church cares, they can excommunicate my services. Besides I have amassed a lot of wealth to take care of my wife, two kids and the poor widow in the house. As for these two elders, Baba will answer that question at question time.

ACT FIVE

SCENE I

A sorcerer's hut. Ngome is standing face to face with the sorcerer. The hut is decorated with some mystical and frightful feathers. Directly above his head are skulls of mortals and wild animals of various kinds.

Baba: Na weti bring you for here today.

Ngome: Baba, it isn't strange to you that you and I have come a very long way. (*Drops a ten thousands francs note*) this is your kola.

Baba: (*sings songs of incantation*) you don talk fine talk. (*Stares at a mysterious pot in front of him*). I di see your enemy them, weti you want make I do with them jes nor.

Ngome: I need some jaz, I mean jaboo to put an end to their existence.

Baba: Na which one you want, silencer one week or silencer one day.

Ngome: Silencer one week. I must spare myself from any trace of suspicion. I want them to die gradually as I did to that pastor who thought he is a hard nut to crack.

Baba: (*Sings song of incantation*) No palava no dey for weti you di ask-am. (picks up a substance from a pot). This jaboo na expert for weti you wan do. Use – am as you don di doam for the other mbutuku them – wey them stand for your road. After one week, you go tell me good news.

Ngome: Trust me, I will do it the same way I did in the previous cases. May the almighty God bless you with disastrous iniquities.

Baba: Thank you my pikin.

Ngome: And, may your miserable life end up in absolute calamity. (*smiles*)

Baba: Thank you plenty for all this blessing them. Thank you my pikin.

Exit Ngome.

Baba: My big big papa them, eye wey i no di lock for night, nawuna kola this (pours palm wine on the ground). Hey! (pause) Na weti I don duam so. Chai, anyhow wey i happen, I just pray say make he take heart. Any ting wey i meet-up man pikin be equal to the man pikin. No matter weti eyes them see-am, them no go vomit blood. (*Sings*).

Exit.

SCENE II

The Pastor's office. Three transparent glasses are seen on a small table placed at the centre of the office. Ngome unfolds a reddish bundle containing a bloody substance and drops the substance in two of the three glasses on the table.

Ngome: (*raising the poisonous glasses*). These six-feet will take good care of them. Dead women don't talk.

> *There is a knock at the door. Enter 1st and 2nd Elders.*

2nd Elder: (*In a calm voice*) Sango, we received a letter from you.

Ngome: Good evening and welcome.

1st Elder: What do you want from us this time around, haven't you done enough harm.

Ngome: (*embracing them*) please calm down and sit down. The Bible says we should not repay evil for evil. I know what you are going through, believe me I am deeply sorry for the pains I put both of you through. (*kneels*) Please forgive me for I know not what came over me.

The two Elders become pathetic towards Ngome. They reach out to him as tears flow down their cheeks.

Ngome: There is of course no doubt about my virtuous love towards you. I am going to lift you to another level in life. (*to 1st Elder*) you will become the next chairlady of the church and you (*pointing at 2nd Elder*) the church treasurer.

> *Both Elders put on a smiling face.*
> *Ngome opens a cupboard and brings out a plastic bottle of cocacola. After filling these glasses with the coke, Ngome serves the poisoned drinks to the Elders. 2nd Elder hastily drinks hers while 1st Elder drinks part of hers and places the glass on the table.*

Ngome: By this time next month, I will joyfully announce your promotions.

1st Elder: Me too.

> *Both Elders start coughing aloud. It becomes so alarming to the extent that they fall to the ground, holding their stomachs and necks as they cough out foam.*

2nd Elder: Sango why! Look at those helpless children of mine. How can you render them orphans at such an age. You are really the devil's incarnate.

1st Elder: My stomach! My stomach. I am dying oh, I am dying oh. I am dying. (*grabs Ngome's leg*) Sango why, didn't you love me as you have always promised me?

Ngome: I love you, it is the devil's work.
(*As if he is in a dream world*)
Baba has finished me. Baba has finished me, Baba has finished me.
(*Picks up 1st Elder's glass*)
Ngome Paulus. I cannot face the world out there. I cannot. Oh greed, greed, oh greed has sent me to an early grave. (*Drinks the poisoned drink*) Good bye Ngome Paulus.

Ngome falls to the ground and screams. His loud cry captures Fomum's attention who is on his way to Ngome's office.

Fomum: Ngome, Elder, what is happening here. (*Touching the Elders, Fomum realizes they now exist in the immortal realm*). What just like that.

Ngome: (*in a dying tone*) Fomum

Fomum: Yes dear.

Ngome: Greed has killed me. Oh Fomum, I should have taken your advice and that of my mother and school teacher. I am a disgrace to humanity. I embezzled church funds, committed sexual immorality with all those who are willing to collaborate with me, and killed Pastor Abel Naboth, these two elders... Take care of my family and pray for my soul.

Fomum: Please don't be pessimistic. There are people who did worst crimes than yours and were forgiven of them all.

Ngome: Can God ever forgive me. Oh the prophecies of my father and school teacher have come to pass in my life. I am a finished man.

Fomum: (*pampering him*) No you are not.

Ngome: We do not feed fowls on market days. Kindly beg my family members to forgive me; I am a disgrace to them.

Fomum: The first person Jesus went to Heaven with is a criminal. Your case is not the worst.

Ngome: The fare of these two Elders will soon lead me to their destination.

Fomum: What! Please repeat this prayer after me. "Lord Jesus forgive me of my sins".

Ngome: (*in a dying voice*) Lord Jesus forgive me of my sins.

Fomum: I have sinned against you and deserve your judgment.

Ngome: I have sin against you and deserved your. (*Chocks, groans, in Fomum's hands and dies*).

Fomum: Ngome, Ngome (*crying*) Oh God….

Exit.

SCENE III

Ngome's residence. Mechane is putting on a very big black gown with a white Lion cloth tied round her waist. Her whole being reflects someone who has been weeping for hours.

Fomum: Nyango Pastor.

Mechane: Your friend has finished us-oh! Your friend has finished us oh. (*Sneezes out a thick mucus*). I never knew I was married to an Iscariot. Oh Ngome, wherever you are, it shall not be well with you.

Fomum: Take it easy please, Ngome says you all should forgive him and restore him to your heart.

Mechane: The worst of it is that he has been excommunicated by the church.

Fomum: What! Excommunicated! He is already a dead man and need not be treated as such. Your husband is a pastor and must be buried as one.

Mechane: (*crying*) Is that what matters Fomum, is that what matters. Being an abominable pastor is worse than ever becoming one. Truly, what an old woman sees while lying in her hut, a young man will never see even if he climbs an iroko. The words of my mother-in-law are still fresh in my mind.

Enter Ma Ewane.

Ma Ewane: (*crying*) How can I bear it? How can I face this gloomy world? I must complete the triangle. Oh Ngome you have killed an old woman before her time.
Takes out a bottle of garmalin 240 and drinks to the last drop

Mechane: Mama what are you doing.

Ma Ewane: The loneliness is unbearable. Take care of Ngome's family.

Mechane: No mama, no, no noooo…

Ma Ewane falls to the ground. As if in a dream world, Mechane and Fomum struggle to bring her back to life, it's too late, Ma Ewane is already on the other side of the bar.

Exit.

SCENE IV

Muan-mbong Quarter Tombel Town. The M.P's residence. The compound is a miniature of paradise, with beautiful glass tiles on the floor and all over the place. The M.P is sitting in front of his house, reading a newspaper title "Jeune Afrique Economie". There is a bottle of Champaign standing on a side stool beside him, with a glittering inscription called "Napoleon".

X-Minister: nhon, this world has become hot and even hotter.

M.P.: What do you mean? I am just coming from NGOLA.

X-Minister: Anyway, how was your session?

MP: It was very scanty, people and people all over the place

X -Minister. Pastor Ngome Paulus is dead.

M.P (*Jeune Afrique Economie falls from his hands*). Are you serious about what you are saying?

X-Minister: yes I am.

M.P: Chai, the hawk has finally picked up tortoise.

X-Minister: Don't worry, the burial will take place this afternoon at 3.pm. Cameroon time.

M. P: Who is responsible for his death?

X-Minister: Have you forgotten we are all strangers in town. See you at the funeral.

M.P: Chai, life is fall of surprise. Pastor Ngome Paulus Ewane of all people... the son of the brain behind my successes... an influential man of God of our generation to be buried with his mother on the same day. Truly, there is nothing to boast of in this world. The drunk's words were really wise sayings. I will follow the drunk's advice, act like Zacheus by giving half my wealth to the poor. A candle loses nothing by lighting another candle. Chai. Lord forgive me for being a man of myself and pretending to be a "MAN OF THE PEOPLE".

SCENE V

At the funeral. Pa Ewane's compound is crowded with Cameroonians from every region and category. Two huge coffins are placed on the table standing at the centre of the compound. At the east side of the compound there are two huge graves and heaps of soil besides them. Ngome's wife and innocent kids are sitting on a bench beside the coffins Fomum is also sitting beside them.

Girl: Good evening my dear brothers and sisters, well-wishers sympathizers and friends. You are all welcome to the burial of Pastor Ngome Paulus Ewane and his mother Mama Ewane Antoinette.

M.P: (*whispers to X-Minister*) Is she going to conduct the funeral service? I can't find any clergy around this place.

X-Minister: Ngome have been excommunicated from the church. May be that damsel standing there is going to do what a grand homme de Dieu is supposed to do.

Girl: Please, permit me read a brief biography of the deceased.

Ngome Paulus Ewane was born on the 31st day of February 1966 in Douala. After obtaining his Teachers Grade II Certificate, he taught as a primary school teacher in G.S Akwaya and G.S Tombel Town. Resigning from teaching, he became a Rev. Pastor to amend his status in life. This new service of his was short lived, as the cold hands of death took him to an untimely and everlasting retirement. His mother's biography could not be traced because the thunder storm of death has drowned every record to be remembered of them. May their souls rest in Peace.

Mourners: Amen.

Girl prays a short prayer, begging God to protect Fomum as he ministers to the audience.

Fomum: Ladies and Gentle, I will like to thank the Ewane's family for giving me an opportunity to share the word of God here today. I was never trained in Theology or Philosophy. I have never in my life attended any Bible School nor School of Theology. I was trained as a teacher of the primary school, with the goal of building the morals and academic foundations of future rulers and leader of this beloved nation and the world at large. With a little encounter I had with God in his word, I plead for your kind attention to listen to what I discovered about God and His creation. I will like us to open our Bibles and read from Genesis chapters 6:5 and 6.

Boy stands up and reads aloud.

Boy: "And God saw how great man's wickedness on earth has become, that every inclination of the thoughts of his heart was only evil all the time. The Lord regretted why he made man on earth and his heart was filled with pain".

Boy seats down

Fomum: Man's wicked thoughts are opposing to God's holiness. Man's sinful thoughts are a problem to the heart of God. Sin is like a knife pierced into God's heart. God feels pain and is the greatest sufferer of all sins. That is why God has decided that every person who actively lives in sin will go to hell when he dies. Every sinful soul will suffer God's judgment in hell. Every sinful soul will suffer God's judgment in hell. Christianity is not a matter of going to church or belonging to a particular church, it is a matter of abandoning sin and abandoning it forever. Failure to do so, be ready to land in the waiting hands of hell when you die.

Pauses and look at the audience with a smile on his face.

When we turn away from our sins and turn to God, we will receive from Him forgiveness of sin, love, kindness, peace and the Holy Spirit of God which will help us fight the devil's schemes of disunity and egotism in our midst. It is only the fear of God that can reconcile us to God, our dead conscience and fellow human beings. Without this, man will never know peace with God, fellow human beings and his conscience. Egotism will then became the master of our lives, causing us to live at war with God, our consciences, our country men and fellow mortals. Life is like a football game, with an entry and an exit. Everything on planet earth is vanity upon vanity. No doubt, God used King Solomon to prove to us that naked we shall go back and we are chasing wind in the guise of fame and riches. We must revitalize our consciences to stimulate and project the vestiges of our virtue. With such, altruism and communalism will defeat egocentrism and greed in our midst, causing us to live at peace with God and fellow human beings such that holiness will blend with virtue to pave our way to paradise when we cross the border of this mortal world.

Praise the Lord

Mourners: Amen.

X – Minister: Amen.

Boy: Let's open our funeral programs and sing song number eleven after which Ijengele, Ngome's intimate friend will say a world of consolation.

Everyone with the funeral program clasp in singing the dirge.

Chorus:
You are an Eagle in this world oh.

You are a Vulture in this world
You are a Parrot-sparrow in this world oh
You are a Pelican or a Dove
There's only one thing you must know

Chorus:

To dust man must return; man must return
Oh to the dust eh

Soloist:

There's only one thing you must know

Chorus:

To dust man must return; man must return
Oh to the dust eh

Soloist:

You are a Lion in this world Oh
You are a Tortoise in this world
You are a Python in this world oh
You are a Chameleon or a Lamb
There's only one thing you must know

Chorus:

To dust man must return; man must return
Oh to the dust eh he he he.

Ijengele: Ngome Paulus Ewane was a very a
hardworking man ever since his youth.
Ngome had five problems in this life. His first
problem was to take care of himself. The
second came up when he got married, and the

third his first son. The fourth and fifth problems were his two daughters. Na condition make njanga hi back bend. Ijengele has made his point.

Some able mourners carry the coffins and drop them in the final destination for mortal body. Fomum pours a spade of dust to each of the graves as he reads from Genesis chapter 3:19.

Fomum: "For you were made from dust, and to dust you must return".

There is weeping from mourners and sympathizers. Burial.

THE END

GLOSSARY

Amuan	my child
Epebuamor	welcome
Kwangkwalang	Bakossi traditional dish
Mbale	I swear
Taaku	tobacco—snuff
Waka soffi	go in peace
Kaya	marijuana
Repe	father (also used for some young men)
Mboko	proliteriat (paupers of the society)
Lewa	school
Mileid	teacher
Chop	food
Mimbo	drink
Wuna	everybody
Flop	full
Wey	who
Plenti	much
Alum	debts
Atog	poverty
Ebume	umbrella
Eboma	bad luck
Nhon	chief----title man
Nyamkusu	horsemeat
Nyamnguu	pork
F.S.L.C	First School Leaving Certificate
Ndume	the back of a tree used as medicine
Kaka mulena	be courageous
Ekoke	cocoyam bread, cake
Nyake	banana
Kumbaly	in pride

Mimbo house	beer parlour
Choko	bribery
Weti	what
Jes-nor	right away
Jaz,jaboo	dangerous and poisonous medicine
Palava	problem
Mbuluku	fools
Nawuna	this is your
Man pikin	man
See am	see
Ngola	Yaounde
Il grido	a cry
Capestata	downtrodden
Obstacles	meat and fish
Diese	sit down
Njangi house	meeting point of a social group
Bulo	work
Diob	God
Mokussa	widow
Makossa	a particular dance using the waist
Instruct	marijuana
Ngombe	an animal that is deaf
wusai	where